Burned
Bricks

*A message of hope for a wounded
generation ready to give up.*

For copies of this book contact:
GONCIL, Inc.
Post Box 323
Merrick, NY 11566
USA

This book is dedicated to my mother, who refused to give up on me when I was struggling, who held on to the conviction that God can use a burned brick for His glory.

Table of Contents

Acknowledgements

I gratefully acknowledge the help of the following people who made this book possible in this form: My wife Mercy, for putting up with me while I chase my convictions, Nisha, my daughter, for proof reading the text and giving me suggestions, Dr. Paul Lutchman and Dr. Wynne Lewis, two people who have considerably influenced me in my development as a Christian leader, for writing introductions to this book and also for their personal friendship. My special thanks to Wilfred Laurent, on whom myself and our church often call for graphic designs, for designing the cover. I am also grateful to Creatspace.com, a division of Amzon.com, for making my dream of publishing this book a reality.

Above all, all glory goes to my Heavenly Father, who chose to use a burned brick from an unknown village in India for the expansion of His kingdom.

"This is an inspiring book. A much needed book. One that I wish was around when I was a young believer battling with all kinds of difficulties. It would have saved me many a heartache. I wish it was available when I started in the ministry. It would have helped me to overcome inferiority complex and believe that the Lord wanted to use a bruised reed.

We owe a great debt to Dr. Sunny for baring his heart and teaching winning principles. I heartily commend it."

-Dr. Wynne Lewis,
Ex General Overseer,
Elim Pentecostal Fellowships,
United Kingdom.

"Dr Sunny Philip speaks from a wealth of experience. He utilizes everyday experiences to unleash heavenly truths. Those that are 'limping' in the Kingdom will find that our Lord and Savior Jesus Christ is the Divine Healer of every situation. Our obedience to His Lordship will enable us to walk in the fullness of life. "Building with Burnt Bricks" is truly a message of hope to a lost and dying world!

Thank you Dr Sunny for an inspiring and 'up to date' book that will have a rippling effect in the Kingdom of God!"

Dr. Paul Lutchman
President - Christian Revival Centre & Jesus for Africa
Vice-Chancellor - Teamwork Bible College International

Something beautiful, something good
All my confusion He understood
All I had to offer Him was brokenness and strife
But he made something beautiful of my life

If there ever were dreams
That were lofty and noble
They were my dreams at the start
And hope for life's best were the hopes
That I harbor down deep in my heart
But my dreams turned to ashes
And my castles all crumbled, my fortune turned to loss
So I wrapped it all in the rags of life
And laid it at the cross.

-Bill Gaither

Preface

Why did I write a book like this?

Two years ago I was invited to moderate a session in a national Christian conference. The session was for youth who had gone through physical, verbal and sexual abuse. I was told that they expected about a hundred youth to show up. One of the leaders was an ex-member of my church and I accepted their invitation. To our surprise, that morning session drew a crowd of over six hundred. I am sure some came just out of curiosity. But hundreds of them were real people who were hurting and seeing their lives as 'burned bricks.' They were scarred for life by something in the past and wondered if they are of any use to anyone anymore.

It turned out to be a difficult session for myself. At first, I had no plans to open up the wounds of my own childhood. I was going to be a Pastor, a leader and a moderator there and nothing more. But witnessing the real sorrow reflected in the faces of so many hundreds of youth, I could not but open up to them at the end of the session. The next few days were very difficult for me as I was forced to relive some of the bad memories of my own childhood.

As I prayed for a healing touch from God, He put the ideas presented in this book in my mind. It is the reason for opening this book with an autobiographical chapter and ending it with a chapter on childhood traumas. Many of the chapters are based on the lessons God has been teaching me over the years. At that time I did not know that Holy Spirit was ministering to me and through me to others. It is my sincere prayer that this book will minister life to you, bring healing to you and strengthen you to move on in life and reach your God given destiny.

At least some established Christians may think that what I have embraced is a liberal interpretation of grace in some chapters. That concern held me back from publishing this book for a while. After re-reading many times some of the chapters that may evoke that concern, I am comfortable with them now. It is true that just a few years ago I did not look at the Bible characters mentioned in those chapters the same way. But then, as a minister, I was still under the influence of an unfair system of reference that held Biblical characters as super giants whereas we were feelings crawling in the mud. The most liberating moment for me was when I was ready to admit that *life is a process*. Most of the characters in the Bible had to go through that process before they became who God wanted them to be. This book is written to provide every single person alive in our generation the hope that they also can endure the process and become who God want them to be.

Chapter One

The Origins

You will understand and appreciate the background of this book, after you read this chapter. It comes straight from my heart. Let me explain.

In 1986, when God started dealing with my life to get into ministry, I refused. I told Him that there is no way He could use a person like me in ministry. It was too late!

I remember the days when the love of God first became real in my life. I was a thirteen year old poor village boy in Kerala, India. That year became so special in my life. Everything changed after I took baptism. All of a sudden there was a well spring of God's love in my heart. I wanted everyone to know the same God and His Son Jesus Christ. I became very active in the youth group in our village church. I started giving small exhortations in youth meetings. Pretty soon I was preaching in open air meetings conducted in bus stops and village markets. I wanted to see the whole world saved.

My relationship with God in those days was so liquid, so pure. I never prayed the religious prayer. I just talked to my heavenly Father. There were two miracles done in my house during that time. One was in the life of one of my younger brothers. He had polio initially and after he started walking with a limp, he fell from a ridge and hit his head on a rock that caused him to have epileptic seizures. One night it got worse. He was having scizures every five minutes. The severity of it was weakening his body right before our eyes. Finally it came to a point where the adults in the village started murmuring about his impending death. I overheard one uncle saying that they will stay in the house through the night, since my brother will not make it to the morning. I was heart-broken. I slipped into my bed and started crying. I remember telling my heavenly Father, if I have a right to live, my brother also has a right to live and so please let him live. I repeated the same sentence and cried myself to sleep. The next morning when I woke up, the house was empty and my brother was sitting in his bed!

I remember another night when many Christian adults in the village came to my house. My mother was in hospital and the news got back to the village that she was on the verge of death. So they came to sing and pray. We children were kept out of the loop, but I overheard an elderly person whispering to another about the impending death of my mother. I again slipped into my bed and started bargaining with my heavenly Father. I asked Him to let my mother live until I graduated from high school. I was in eighth grade at that time. In those days, the high school graduation was after the tenth grade. I was good in studies and was going to be the first person to go to college from our immediate families. It was a big dream of my mother to see me go to college. So I wanted God to extend her life for three years to see me getting into a college. I told Him that he could take her after that, if He wanted. God again answered my prayers and delivered her. She recently crossed the eighty year mark!

Because of my close relationship with my heavenly Father, I decided to go into ministry. Since my childhood I had public speaking skills and I started getting awards in that area since the age of fourteen. I was going to use this God given talent for His glory. I knew what I would do. I would attend college for two years for a Pre- Degree program and then enroll into a good Bible College for a degree in theology and serve God all my life.

But it did not turn out that way. At the end of my second year of college, when our families found out that I was planning to join a Bible College, they were not pleased. I was the first born, was good in studies and had the best prospect of getting ahead in life. So they all wanted me to continue my college education and land a good job and take care of the family. Though I had the Bible College application all filled out, it was never mailed in. I surrendered to pressure and decided to continue the college education.

It had an unexpected result in my life. All of a sudden my thinking changed. I concluded that if I am not going to be a minister, I do not have to live a perfect life. I could enjoy my youth just like my friends. And I started doing it by hanging out with my fiends more and sneaking into movie theatres etc. Then it got worse.

I was eighteen when I came across the book, "Why I Am Not a Christian" by Bertrand Russell in the college library. I started reading it and it shook the foundations of my faith. I ran to the village preachers to find answers for his arguments against Christianity. But they could not answer them. Most of them did not even have high school education. I became frustrated after one year and concluded with Russell that religion is a crutch for weak people and it is simply a set up for some to make a living. In the same college where at age seventeen I used to lead the boys' prayer group, at age twenty I was an atheist. I was totally lost and trying to emulate the hippy life style that I came across in magazines (with the exception of the sex and drug aspects).

It took a direct intervention from God to redirect my path. But even after giving up on atheism and rationalism, I was not the same person that I used to be. My thinking had changed. When I was sheepishly re-embracing Christianity, it was purely cerebral. It did not have the warmth of a personal relationship. I had slipped into youthful foolish ways during my bracket period and was still a slave of it. The purity of my life was gone.

By the grace of God, I came to the USA in 1977 after my marriage. By then, becoming a minister was the last thing on my mind. I was a struggling Christian at best. I still had intellectual qualms about many things in the church. Occasionally I struggled severely like a drug addict having a relapse. But I kept it to myself. In 1981, when I took the initiative to form a Christian youth organization for the Indian Christian immigrants in New York called PYFA, it was for my sake also. I knew we would be spiritually gone in this country in no time, if we did not have support mechanisms. But I was getting closer to God slowly at the same time.

I just wanted to study, find a good job and live the American dream in a suburb somewhere. I graduated with a B.S. in Chemical Engineering from Polytechnic University in New York in a year when people in this field were being laid off by the thousands. I took a job I could find since my wife was pregnant with our son. Then in 1986, things went haywire in my life again.

God started calling me into ministry again! It was so specific and so real. But I could not say yes. How could God use a man who was so close to Him in childhood yet slipped away into atheism? How could He forgive a person who had filled out the application form to join a Bible College but never mailed it? How could He use a person who used to live a pure life knowing that his future is in ministry and then allowed himself to slip into the sins of the world? I said no.

But He would not leave me alone. I remember a six month period when the spirit of God was so heavy on me that I would be crying inexplicably. God would bring even the smallest sins I had committed to my memory and along with it would come a huge sense of shame and a spirit of repentance. Before my brain had time to act, my heart would slip into a repentance mode and would ask God forgiveness for it, tears running down my cheeks. It was like someone else was in charge of my life. (Actually it was. I did not know at that time that Holy Spirit was leading me through a deep cleansing to use me again).

Then God taught me lessons from the life of Jonah, Jacob and Peter and showed me how he would not give up on people whom He plans to use. I realized for the first time that God is a God of second chances. I had not heard such messages in the legalistic churches that I grew up in.

After a long battle, I could slowly begin to accept His love and forgiveness. I realized that even when He was ready to forgive me, I was not ready to forgive myself. I had this huge weight of guilt and shame on me that I carried around for years even after accepting His call.

In 1986, when I started ministering in my local church in New York, my prayer was that my ministry would not go beyond that. I did not want to be famous, I did not want any credits, I did not even want anyone to know that I was doing 'ministry.' But to my surprise, God began to open doors for me. Before long, I was on the radio in New York and ministering in youth conferences across USA and even internationally. I remember the heaviness on my heart as I prepared for those meetings. Many times the shame of my past failures would be so heavy on me that I would feel like a phony. I questioned my worthiness to minister to others. I had to totally depend on God's grace to minister and He always came through.

I had to learn many of the lessons in this book myself. These are passages and stories and messages that God gave me to minister to my own spirit and thereafter to others. These are thoughts that finally brought inner healing to me. Even now occasionally I get under the weight of my past. But I am not a slave to it anymore. I have learned since then that God is not ashamed of the burned marks on the bricks that He uses to build His edifice called the church.

It is my prayer that these thoughts will bring inner healing to you as well and make you whole again. I hope it will transform you as it did in my life and give you the confidence to pick up the pieces and move on into your destiny with the help of our heavenly Father.

Chapter Two

From Street to Center stage

Jesus was sitting for dinner at a rich Pharisee's house. Things had surely changed. Pharisees used to hate Jesus. They considered him a trouble maker. Eventually they were instrumental in his crucifixion. Yet, here was Jesus in a Pharisee's house.

One can try to figure out why Simon, a Pharisee would invite Jesus for dinner. Luke tells us that he was a leper. Probably he was hoping Jesus would realize his condition and would heal him like many other lepers. Perhaps he was impressed by the following Jesus had by then. Wherever he went, hundreds followed him to receive their healing and people were paying attention to every word he uttered. Simon probably had a few questions of his own.

But things took a different turn that day. When the story unfolds, the first thing we learn is that Simon did not go all out to receive Jesus- it was more a half hearted reception. We learn that he violated one of the cherished signs of hospitality in their culture.

People usually traveled by foot those days and after they walked along the dusty roads of Palestine, it was customary for people to take their sandals off and to wash their feet before they went inside the house. (This is the same in many of the Eastern cultures even today). In Palestine of Jesus' day, the rich would always send out a slave to wash the feet of the guests and to wipe them with a towel. If the man was not rich enough to have slaves, he would go out himself and wash the feet of the guests. Simon was a rich man, but he did not send out any slaves to wash the feet of Jesus or his disciples. It was an intentional slight. Neither did he go out and offer the kiss of peace. Probably he wanted to leave a little room to justify himself if he received his healing and could move into the inner circle of his friends again. "Yeah, I may have given him a dinner so that he would heal me, but certainly it was not a sign of accepting him or his claims in anyway!"

We learn from history that in those days, wealthy people always made their home in an open courtyard, with plenty of open space and huge front yards. It was common to leave the dining room open and to let others come to the front yard and listen in on the dinner conversation. Especially when a well known teacher or philosopher was the guest of honor, many would flock the front yard to hear his words of wisdom.

Here was Jesus and his disciples at this wealthy home. Certainly the news had moved fast in the village and many had gathered to listen to him. All of them were welcome at Simon's house- except the woman who was a burned brick.

We can picture the scene in our mind like this. Jesus was naturally given the place of honor with his disciples surrounding him on either side. At the other place of honor was the host, Simon, basking in the glory of the moment. For the disciples, who mostly came from poor backgrounds, it was a recognition and honor to be invited to a wealthy home and given places of honor. So probably they were all jostling for the best spot, the spot that had the highest visibility, so that the people could see them well.

Then another person entered into the picture uninvited. A woman entered in to a male only audience. She started taking unprecedented liberty with Jesus, violating all social customs of the day.

She was not trying to crash the party. She was not an attention grabber. She did not want to be in the lime light. She just wanted to get to the feet of Jesus! So she slipped in totally unnoticed until she landed herself at the feet of Jesus. Tears of gratitude were already running down her cheeks.

She started shedding them on the feet of Jesus and wiping his feet with her own hair. She probably heard the despicable way

Simon received Jesus and wanted to right the wrong. She just did it the way she knew how.

Yet, it was just the beginning. She had come prepared to go all out that day to worship Jesus. She opened the small bottle tied to a string around her neck and the fragrance of it was unmistakable. It was spikenard, which would cost up to 300 pence per bottle. (One penny was the salary for a common laborer for a day's work). A whole year's salary for one act of worship!

As the fragrance of the perfume began to fill the room, along came the reactions. Simon could not believe that a woman had shown the courage to violate the protocol in his house (though he himself was the first one to violate them). Simon started questioning Jesus. How can he allow this sinner woman to touch him? Pharisees only allowed their moms, wives or daughters to touch them or get closer to them. No one else could even wash their clothes! Yet, here was Jesus, who claimed his righteousness exceeded that of Pharisees, allowing a total stranger to touch his feet, wipe his feet with her own hair and spread perfume all over him. Plus, if he is a prophet like he claims to be, how come he did not realize that it is a notorious sinner woman? Even if what she did was an act of worship, she was unworthy in Simon's vocabulary.

Even more astounding was the response from the disciples: *"What a waste!"* They were with Jesus, but they did not believe in going all out in worship. They were like most of the modern day Christians. Their worship was just cerebral. They reasoned that it probably cost her one hundred days wages to purchase that bottle of perfume. She might have spent everything she had for that act of worship. Why waste so much money for one act of worship?

Let us look at this again to see the differences. Simon was a self righteous sinner. He could not understand the heart of Jesus. He did not even know his own heart. He certainly did not know the heart of the woman! He misunderstood Jesus as a false prophet, himself as a saint and the woman as a sinner that cannot be saved. In short, Simon responded to Jesus with his mind. The woman on the other hand was a repentant sinner. She understood Jesus as someone who had totally forgiven her, herself to be forgiven and the value of forgiveness. In short, the woman responded to Jesus with her heart.

What interests us is the response from Jesus. He freely acknowledged that the woman was a sinner- a great sinner. He said her 'many sins' have been forgiven. In other words, she was not a sinner now!

This is where the world goes wrong with the burned bricks. They can always remember the days of your struggle, your failure. But for some reason they cannot remember the day Jesus changed your life! They also cannot understand the depth of gratitude from such a heart. They cannot understand why someone will go all out in worshipping God. "Why the tears, why the noise, why spend money, why, why, why?" they ask. Only if they could see things the way Jesus did!

When this woman entered the room, it was not a publicity stunt. It was a natural reaction from a grateful heart. She was oblivious of the surroundings. She did not care for the host or the male crowd in the room. She just wanted to get to the feet of Jesus. He knew that. So He did not reproach her.

What made her the center of attention was not her past, but her present. It was the fragrance of the perfume that caught everyone's attention. What she was carrying with her was not the stench of her past sins, but the sweet aroma of a changed life!

Then Jesus took it one step further. In Matthew and Mark, Jesus promised that wherever the gospel is preached, her story will be mentioned as a memorial for her.

She had moved from the vile streets of Palestine to the center stage in the kingdom of God! This is the promise we carry as burned bricks. The world may continue to focus on our past and declare us unworthy, but our savior has a different take on it. He will not whitewash our past. He may declare to the whole world that our sins are many (thereby exposing our burn marks) but He will also declare to the whole world that 'they are all forgiven." Then He will boldly proclaim that you do not have to stay in the shadows anymore, but can move to the center stage. And God will begin to use you despite your burned marks.

Chapter Three

Building With Burned Bricks

Nehemiah was one of the leaders whom God used to bring the Old Testament Israelites back from the Babylonian captivity. Under his leadership, a third group of people returned to Jerusalem from Babylon. By profession he was a cupbearer to the king of Persia. Then God decided to incorporate Nehemiah in His plans.

Nehemiah had a mission to rebuild the walls of Jerusalem, the city of his forefathers. It was a God inspired mission. Nehemiah walked into it, so to speak.

When he came to Jerusalem with the blessings of the emperor whom he served as the cupbearer, he had nothing much except the vision and a passion burning within him. It was like a fact finding mission. He needed to know 'what his God had put in his heart.' In the night he got up with a few men to get a picture of his life's mission. As they rode around the city on mules, he witnessed the city and its walls in shambles. The land had become a reproach.

He called the Jews together and challenged them to join with him to rebuild the walls of Jerusalem. They were confident that 'the God of heaven Himself would prosper them.'

As soon as they embarked on the project to rebuild the city walls, enemies arose. "What are these feeble Jews doing?" They laughed and despised Nehemiah and his friends.

They had every reason to despise them. Even they knew that the Jews had fallen out of favor with their God. Because of their willful disobedience and refusal to correct their ways, God had given up on them over hundred and seventy years ago. The judgment of God fell on His people. The Babylonians had come and destroyed their land, burned down the capital city of Jerusalem, plundered the Jerusalem temple and burned it to ruins.

After seventy years, a group had returned under the leadership of Zerubbabel and Ezra and had rebuilt the temple, though it was no comparison to the glory of the original temple. But the community that returned was living as peasants with Palestinians and Arabs, much like today and never fully established themselves.

Nehemiah came on the scene almost a hundred years later. Even then the walls were not rebuilt to provide security for the people who lived in the city. The reproach had not been lifted. The inhabitants of the land were extremely poor, powerless and living under the shame and guilt of their past.

When Nehemiah convinced them that God was restoring them and they did not have to live in the shame and loss of the past, people came forward and joined with him in the task of rebuilding the walls. The story given to us in the book of Nehemiah is riveting, to say the least. They finished the project by delegation- each person building a small portion of the wall.

In chapter four we come across their struggles. The first one was mockery. The enemies pointed out correctly that they lacked the resources to fulfill their vision. Israel never accomplished anything because of their abundance. It was always the mercy and provisions of God that helped them in the arid Middle East. Now that they are trying to come back and reestablish themselves, all they could see around them was rubbish- piles of what had been once a prestigious city. In the piles were remnants of the temple of God, where the Shekinah glory of God had descended and remained for generations. The ornate artworks of Solomon's temple lie among the waste. When the Babylonian army set fire to the city, everything had burned down into one undistinguishable heap. Things that had the carving 'holy unto God' lay beside things of no value. There was no separation between common and holy.

Everything equally burned down, everything lying together in a garbage heap.

What Sanballat and his cronies asked was a legitimate question. When all you can see is piles of remnants burned down in the judgment fires of God, how do you rebuild? *"Will they revive stones from the heaps of rubbish- stones that are burned?"*

That is exactly what the Jews did! They dug through the piles and recovered the burned bricks and built the wall with it. I am sure that they used fresh bricks also. But there it was….. fresh bricks and bricks with burned marks all over them side by side on the walls of Jerusalem, bringing glory to God.

This is what we see in the kingdom of God also. If one were to look at this beautiful edifice that God is building up, namely, the church of God, one can see bricks so clean that the angels will be proud of them. Often times, next to them will be bricks with burned marks all over. Sitting next to people who never violated any of the Ten Commandments will be people who broke most of them one time or another. In Paul's letters he makes it very clear. After giving a list of people who live in violation of God's laws, he proclaims, "Such were some of you." 'You were once darkness,' he states elsewhere.

But it is not easy, though. The constant reminder of the past all around you can lead you to discouragement. Dr. Charles Swindoll has pointed out four areas of discouragement from this chapter, three of which are found in the tenth verse and the fourth in the eleventh. These areas are: Loss of strength, loss of vision, loss of confidence and loss of security (<u>Hand Me Another Brick.</u> Nashville, TN: Thomas Nelson, Inc. (1978)

Anyone who has gone through the process can identify with the Jews in the days of Nehemiah. After a while you get tired of digging through the rubbish of your life, even when you know there are bricks (the talents that you once used for the glory of God) there that God can recover and use to rebuild your life. That is the loss of strength.

When people are constantly reminding you of your past, all you will see is the rubbish, not the fact that God has already recovered many bricks albeit their burned marks and is using you for His glory. You get tired of answering people's questions. You get tired of finding explanations for yourself. You begin to lose hope. That is the loss of vision.

Along the way you will be so tempted to give up on yourself. The process is taking too long, you may say. "There is a long way to go before I can reach where God wants me to be again and I don't think I can make it," you may conclude. "It is not working as fast as I expected, so I might as well give up," your mind may whisper. 'There is way too much rubbish piled up in my past. It can never be completely taken care of,' you may tell yourself. That is the loss of confidence.

Then there will be adversaries who are determined to *'come into their midst and kill them and cause the work to cease.'*

They are not excited that you are on the road to restoration. They had taken advantage of you while you were down. It is to their benefit that the status quo remains. So they will attack you, spread stories about you and slander you every which way they can. This may cause you to be gripped with fear and desire to give up. That is the loss of security.

But you cannot give in to the schemes of the enemy. You cannot give up. One day the process will be over. Instead of complaining, thank God for His mercy that He would come down with a spade and sieve through the rubbish of your life to recover the bricks. He who has started a good work in you is able to finish it.

To some the burned brick represent the scars of the godless life they lived for so long. Nicky Cruz, whose story is featured in 'The Cross and The Switchblade,' is a preacher who literally carries marks on his body that is a testimony to his gang days. John Newton owned up to his slave trading past and allowed God to transform him. 'Amazing grace,' the best loved hymn of all times is more than a song. It is a life story of a man who would graciously look at the burned marks on his life and wonder how a holy God would love a wretch like him.

To some the burned brick represent that which was bringing glory to God at one time in their life, but now is gone. It can be a Christian singer who is not singing anymore because of something that happened in his or her life, or a Pastor who is not preaching anymore, or a young person rebounding from a drug habit or a missionary who had to leave the mission field in shame. Your current estate need not be your final estate.

God can still use you. He can restore you. The burned marks will be always visible. But God will restore you to your place in the grand scheme of things. You can still be part of God's work on earth, doing what you were created to do despite the burned marks you carry everywhere with you.

Chapter Four

The Prophet With A Limp

Jacob had a destiny. The problem was that he did not know how he would get there. Neither did his parents. Even the prophecy that 'I have rejected Esau and has chosen Jacob' did not help.

So everyone wanted to help Jacob reach there. His mother thought Jacob would never amount to anything without her help. After all he was a docile young man always hanging around the tent. He was nothing like his brother Esau who was athletic, a famous hunter and well known in the town.

At age sixty five, it looked like he still did not know what to do with his life. He had not married like his brother and started a family. Just taking care of his father's sheep and hanging around the tent was his life.

His mother Rebecca decided to take things into her own hands and to help her beloved son. She came to know about Isaac's plan to bless Esau and give him a double portion of everything he possessed. (It was customary in that culture to give double portion to the first born). She cooked a lamb and made it taste like venison (changed spices, I guess). She covered the hands of Jacob with wool to make it feel like the hairy hands of Esau. She made him go before Isaac with the dish she prepared and pretend to be his brother. The response of Isaac is insightful. "You sound like Jacob, but your hands feel like the hands of Esau." Rebecca did not know that people who lose one sense always develop their other senses further to compensate for it.

Isaac accepted Jacob's explanation and his dish. He was satisfied and blessed Jacob. Though technically he became the possessor of double portion blessings, he never enjoyed it for one day! The same night, fearing an ambush by his angry brother, Jacob ended up running to his uncle's house. *He did not reach his destiny with the help of his mother.*

Along the way at Bethel he had his first encounter with God. Jacob was surprised that God had an interest in him after what he had done. But God's plans are unchangeable and He does not regret about His choices. So God promised to be with Jacob and bring him back to Bethel one day and fulfill all the promises in his life. (Genesis 28:15).

In the turmoil of the hour, Jacob probably did not grasp the depth of those promises, Even though he made oaths before God who appeared to him, he forgot them quickly... For as soon as he reached the house of his uncle Laban, he forgot all about the promises of God. We see him struggling to eek out a destiny for him. In Laban he might have met his equal. But it is a mute point. After fourteen years and two wives and many children, Jacob woke up one day to realize that he has not reached his destiny. In fact he hadn't reached anywhere in life. "When shall I also provide for my own house?" he lamented.

Jacob schemed a way to gain a flock of sheep for himself. He followed a local myth and it worked! But it was not the rods of poplar, almond and chestnut trees that did the trick; it was the hand of God extended to help him, as God made it clear in Genesis 31. However, the worldly establishment of Laban was not interested to see a child of God prosper and Jacob ended up running away again.

Jacob's grandfather Abraham had multiple flocks of sheep. His own father had so many sheep that the land could not contain them. So, Jacob thought possessing multiple flocks of sheep is what would fulfill him also. But he was wrong!

Isn't it funny that every time Jacob got something, he ended up running from it all? The reason was that God had ordained that it was His blessings and plans for him that would make Jacob great.

At the brook of Jabbok, Jacob realized the emptiness of it all. He had flocks of sheep entrusted to each of his sons. (In other words, even the next generation was set financially). He had wives, concubines, servants- everything materially. But Jacob was empty inside. He was finally ready to accept what God had in store for him

He fought with an angel until early morning. It was not a fist fight. It was rather like a child grabbing the dress of its mother and refusing to let go until his or her needs are met. It was a fight of tears and supplication. It was refusing to let go off God until He answered. "I will not let You go unless You bless me."

God had only one demand prior to blessing Jacob. Can you admit where you are in life? How desperately do you aspire for the change? Are you really ready to change? God told him that it would be an identity change. He could not be Jacob (a supplanter) and walk in God's blessings at the same time. God had to restore him. It was going to cost him. God touched the socket of Jacob's hip as a mark of his encounter with God, causing Jacob to limp for the rest of his life. When God realized Jacob was ready, he blessed him and changed his name to Israel (prince of God).

Even then Jacob did not fully accept what God had in store for him. We see him changing plans again. He was on his way to Bethel, which was a wooded place. A man of his dignity and wealth had no reason to go and live in a rural place. So instead, he moved into the expensive suburbs of Shechem. Turmoil, not peace, followed him again. His daughter was date raped there. His sons Levi and Simeon ended up as murderers. The family became such a stench in the neighborhood that Jacob in his old age ended up running away again.

While running away at an elderly age, wondering what in the world is happening to him, he heard God's voice again. Though no one else wanted him then, God still wanted him and reminded Jacob of his promise not to leave him until he comes back to Bethel in peace. Jacob still had a place to go to!

How many times we like Jacob have run away from God's will and God's plan? Along the way we may become rich like Jacob, we may have a family like Jacob, we may become successful like Jacob. Others may enter into our life with advice and guidance (with good intentions). But unless we get to the place where God want us to be, we will never have our peace and finally settle down.

Only after he hit the absolute bottom, when he had no other place to turn, did Jacob accept fully what God had in store for him. His place was in Bethel. When he got there, Jacob became 'Israel,' the prince of God. God would eventually uproot him again and let him die in Egypt, in a position of honor.

Jacob became a burned brick. For the rest of his life, he limped around. When he met his brother Esau, he was limping. When he walked into the palace of Pharaoh, he was limping. But there was a marked difference in him. The grabber became a 'blesser'. He had no problem giving multiple flocks of sheep as a gift to Esau. When he came into the palace of Pharaoh, it was not to see what he could grab from there, but to bless him in the name of Jehovah.

Jacob finally became what he was meant to be- a prophet of God. In Genesis chapter 49 when he blesses his children, he spoke into their life prophetically, even talking about the 'star of Judah' which was a prophecy about Jesus Christ. When he died, it was a peaceful death- no doubts, no regrets, no inner turmoil. Jacob just 'drew his feet into the bed and breathed his last.'

The man who came into the world in tension and turmoil, who lived for much of his life in tension and turmoil, left the earth in perfect peace. How come? He allowed God to build him up though it was as a burned brick.

Chapter Five

Your Children Shall Return

While growing up, I hated the book of Jeremiah. All the messages I had heard from this book were negative. I used to think that it is a book that contained endless lists of punishments from God. Then everything changed one day.

Once I was reading through the entire Bible. Out of necessity, I had to read the book of Jeremiah. I was shocked by what I read! I realized that some of the most poignant messages of God's love and promise for restoration are found in this book.

One of the passages that really ministered to me is the basis of this chapter. It is one of the most beautiful pictures of restoration I have come across in the Bible. Let me explain.

In Jeremiah's days the nation of Israel was going away from their Lord God, Jehovah, much like our society today. God had sent many prophets to correct them. They turned them down and even killed some of them. They stoned some of them. They wanted their freedom to live in any which they pleased. Anyone who objected to that had to be removed from the scene one way or other.

Jeremiah's story is very unique. He did not come from a priestly family. He had no intentions of going into ministry or becoming a prophet. Yet, God called him at a very young age and appointed him as a prophet to his nation. His message was not gladly received, since it was a message of correction. "Why do you want to die in your sins? Turn to God and live"- he would plead to his contemporaries. But they would not listen.

Jeremiah was becoming a burden to that generation. Their nation was still doing well financially. But God through Jeremiah started proclaiming the destruction of that nation. He spoke about Babylonians coming and destroying Jerusalem and taking the Jewish people to Babylon as captives. (Babylon was not an empire at that time). He told the people to 'seek the peace of the city where God is taking them and in its prosperity they will have prosperity.' He spoke it such certainty as if they were around the corner!

People hated this trouble maker. They cussed him, locked him up and even threw him into a pit to drown in mud. It was an Ethiopian slave who had pity on him and saved him from there.

Finally the day came when everything Jeremiah was prophesying came to pass. The Babylonians did come. They burned the city down. They destroyed the beautiful Jerusalem temple. When they chained the young men and women of Judea and marched them to Babylon, Jeremiah was an eyewitness. He was standing in the courtyard of the king with his legs locked to a tree (a way of handling mentally ill people in old days).

I have tried to picture his condition then. How can a prophet bear the full impact of what he had been preaching for forty years? How can he take it when God had given that generation multiple opportunities to turn around and he was the messenger? "Why do you want to die in your sins? Turn to God and live!"- Jeremiah would have recounted all the occasions when he had cried out that message. He could have turned to that generation that declared him crazy and locked his feet into a tree and made a spectacle out of him and murmured, "Don't blame God, you brought this upon yourselves."

Yet instead of wallowing in self pity and sinking into depression, Jeremiah allowed the spirit of God to speak through him yet again. Turning to that long human chain of potential slaves, he cried out, "Don't worry. Your children will return to this land."

What? Is it possible that God would show mercy to a people who had utterly rejected His teaching and corrupted themselves beyond measure? After allowing them to be uprooted from

41

their land and become slaves in a foreign land, God had plans to protect them there and bring their children back? Is restoration possible for a person or community after they mess up so much? Is there no limit to the burn marks a person can bear before God would totally give up on them?

In order to express the full gravity of this, let us divulge into history for a moment. After the time of Solomon, the nation of Israel was divided into two- the southern kingdom being known as Judea and the Northern kingdom being known as Israel. Since Judah was the prominent tribe in Judea, we see the southern kingdom referred to as Judah in the prophetic literature. Similarly, the northern kingdom is referred to as Ephraim in the prophetic literature many times.

The northern kingdom started going away from God based on a political decision. When Jeroboam became the king of the northern kingdom, he knew he had to do certain things to secure his rule. There was only one temple in the land at that time and it was in the southern kingdom of Judea. Jeroboam knew the central place the temple worship had in the life of his subjects. He was afraid that if they went to Jerusalem to worship God there, their hearts could join with them and they may ask for reconciliation and for the people to be reunited. It would cost him his throne!

Therefore he wisely decided to provide alternatives for his people. After all, as a political leader, it was important for Jeroboam to keep the people contended. So he declared two new places of worship and opposed anyone going to Jerusalem to worship. He placed two golden calves, one in Bethel and the other in Dan. (Bethel was the place where their forefather Jacob had the vision of God. Now through a political maneuver, it was declared the headquarters of idol worship!)

In the old days, the idol worship had many other customs attached with it. Sometimes it even led to sacrificing children for blessings from deities (which later happened in Israel) and many times sleeping with the temple prostitutes was a part of the ritual (which also happened in Israel later on).

Just like a ball rolling downhill gains momentum, an intentional departure from God's revealed truth will always plunge a person, a community or a nation into greater vile until the whole system crashes under the mighty force of that momentum.

This is what happened to the northern kingdom. They totally forgot the God of their fathers. They filled their lands with idols. They even entered into heinous crimes like human sacrifice. They eventually became a land of drunkards. Yet, it is amazing to see that many of the great prophets of Israel like Elijah and Elisha ministered in the northern kingdom, which was called Israel, with its capital in Samaria. It was as if God was beckoning them back.

At one point, God prophesied through Isaiah that the northern kingdom would be destroyed in sixty five years. Still they could not turn around. The ball had gained too much momentum. It was going downhill too fast for anyone to stop it. The people were too caught up in their ways that they could not change. None of the dire predictions made by the prophets actually helped them to turn around.

Finally the date in the divine calendar for judgment came. The Assyrians came and mercilessly killed thousands of them. They even split open the pregnant women to kill their babies. They were displaced from their land. Thousands of them were sold in slave markets and eventually got scattered all over the world.

Yet, the southern kingdom did not learn from this lesson. They picked up where the north left off. They plunged into sin without any concern. Violation of God's laws were not a matter of public decry.

Finally, the Day of Judgment came for the southern nation also. The Babylonian army rode into the city of Jerusalem, destroyed it and burned it down and captured all the youth to be taken to Babylon as slaves. As the human chain was slowly moving to Babylon, we see Jeremiah crying out: "Your children will return."

When we read through the book of Jeremiah, we can see a true picture of God as a heart-broken father. The most touching passages are in chapter 31. While decreeing how He would re-gather Israel from all corners of the world, He did not forget to include the northern kingdom. In fact, He declares Ephraim (northern kingdom) to be His firstborn. Also we read, "Is Ephraim My dear son? Is he a pleasant child? For though I spoke against him, I earnestly remember him still. Therefore My heart yearns for him." (v.20).

God is identifying with fathers everywhere who worry over their wayward children. Ephraim certainly was not a 'pleasant child'. He was a very disobedient child. Everything that happened to him was the result of that disobedience. Yet, He could not forget Ephraim.

It is the story of every parent. On one hand they want to let them go. Let the children learn their lesson- whether it is rotting in a jail cell or suffering from sicknesses they got directly as a result of their lifestyle. On the other hand, the same parents' hearts melt at the plight of their children.

In fact, there is a secret revealed in this chapter. In verse 15, we see a woman crying for her children. Her name is Rachel. Ephraim was Rachel's grandson (down the line). So here we have a grandmother crying for her generations. It is said that she 'refused to be comforted.' How can she?

It is easy for others to give up on your children. It is easy for the 'system' to lock them up and throw the key away. It is easy for all the old friends to move on. But how can you as a parent? Don't you remember all the dreams you had about this child- how this child was going to grow up and be good and get your family respect and position in society?

Then it all went downhill. It started with petty things. But before anyone could turn the child around, it escalated into bigger things and now they were facing the consequences.

What are the options for the parents? Loving parents will never give up on their children. I see proof of that in the lives of grandparents bringing up the children of incarcerated men and women. I see it in grandmothers, mothers and siblings waiting in line patiently outside barbed wires to get a few minutes with their loved ones in jail cells. I see it in countless loved ones trying to catch a few minutes of sleep in hospital waiting rooms. They 'refused to be comforted.' They refuse to give up, when others give up. They refuse to forget when others forget. They refuse to surrender to despair. They do the only thing they can.....cry, cry and cry again.

But God promises that their tears are not in vain. "Thus says the LORD; Refrain your voice from weeping, and your eyes from tears; for your works shall be rewarded, says the Lord. ...There is hope in your future, says the Lord, that your children shall come back to their own border." (v.16, 17).

Yes, parents and grandparents and loved ones. Don't be ashamed of the burned marks on your dear ones. God can still restore them and use them. So, be hopeful. Just do your part. 'Your works shall be rewarded', says the Lord. "Your children shall come back to their own border."

Chapter Six

The Blinded Apostle

It was high noon by the time the party had reached the city gates of Damascus. They had traveled all the way from Jerusalem to finish the business. There was a very educated young man named Saul who was the leader of the band. But it was not his education that gave him the leadership role now. In fact, you would not expect an educated man to get involved in the type of things this band was doing. They were in the murdering business. They even had the approval of the big honchos in Jerusalem. But that did not make it right.

They were a passionate band of vigilantes. A serious challenge had risen up against their religion. A new group of people had come on the scene who were challenging their culture and customs and heritage. They called themselves Nazarenes. These humble folks had the audacity to claim that a person whom their leaders had handed over to the Romans to be crucified, had resurrected on the third day and that he had ascended to the heavens, thereby proving that he did in fact come from the heavens.

Someone had to do something about it. This group was making inroads in to their community. More than five thousand people had already joined them. And they were spreading to surrounding nations like Syria.

Generally you would not expect a well groomed, educated young man like Saul, born in a rich family in Tarsus and educated in the best schools of the day to join a vigilante group and become a hit man. But the passion for his cause was burning in him and he was determined to do something about this sect that was causing havoc in his community.

That day he had come with some of his friends to Damascus, Syria for the same reason. He wanted to search out followers of this new sect and arrest them under a religious edict and drag them back to Jerusalem to stand trial before the Sanhedrin. They had very successfully orchestrated the death of a leader of this sect named Stephen, which had emboldened them. In fact, Saul was an eye witness to that crime and was directly involved in the planning and execution.

Everything looked smooth and trouble free until a bright light flashed upon them. Being in the Middle East, it was easy to think of it as a sun stroke (for it was not a rainy day and what they witnessed was not a lightning). This flash was immediately followed by a roar that sounded like a thunder, which was highly unusual. All the members of Saul's party covered their faces with their tunic. They were clearly panic stricken.

To their surprise, Saul started talking to the thunder. "Who are you, Lord?" asked Saul.

The band heard another thunder. They could not decipher anything. But Saul asked again, "What do you want me to do, Lord?"

The band again heard another thunder. Then it was all over.

Except that Saul was blind now. The leader needed help now to walk. He told his friends to take him to the house of a man named Judas, on a street named Straight. He said he had to receive more instructions for his life from Jesus Christ!

His friends could not believe their ears. They had come to Damascus to arrest the followers of Jesus. Now their leader wanted to receive instructions from him? Besides, for them this Jesus was crucified and dead months ago. How was this dead man now going to give directions to Saul? They left their leader at Judas' house and went back to Jerusalem.

Saul was a young man who was in charge of his life. Everyone could see that he would rise up to a leadership position in the community. His opposition to the Christians had made him noteworthy. But now, he claimed that Jesus would send someone to him with instructions for his future.

Waiting in the house of Judas, Saul felt helpless. His blindness forced him to seek the help of others, which was not his style. Besides, no one showed up with instructions. But something had changed within him. He had a peace. He was no longer impatient. He had an iron clad confidence that Jesus was sending someone with instructions.

Finally after three days, a man named Ananias showed up. He also claimed he had instructions from Jesus about Saul and was directed specifically to the house where he was staying. Not that Ananias wanted to. Saul's reputation had preceded him to Syria. He was a troublemaker. But Jesus wanted him! He told Ananias that Saul is a 'chosen vessel,' a phrase that was used to refer to prophets.

When the two met, there were no surprises. It was as if a mutual friend had introduced the two very well. As soon as he entered the room, Ananias called Saul 'brother.' The animosity and hatred that had been at the root of this hesitant meeting had been lifted. Ananias prayed for Saul's sight to return and something like scales fell from his eyes and he received sight.

Saul of Tarsus did receive instructions from Jesus and later became Apostle Paul. He wrote two third of the New Testament. His writings are still impacting the lives of billions.

Saul did not know that he had become a burned brick that day. Even though he received sight that day, Bible scholars believe that he had issues with eye sight for the rest of his life. Later in one of his letters he wrote, "See, with what large letters I have written to you with my own hand." (Galatians 4:11). In the same letter Paul says again: "For I bear witness that, if possible, you would have plucked out your own eyes and given them to me."(Galatians 4:15). These passages make it clear that the Galatians knew about the issues Paul had with his eyesight.

As an apostle, he was well known for the miracles that had taken place by his hands. In Corinth and in Ephesus, many miracles had happened by his hands. Sometimes 'unusual' miracles had taken place his ministry. (Acts 19:11).

Yet, Paul was not healed himself. Listen to his own words: "Concerning this thing, I pleaded with the Lord three times that it might depart from me. And He said to me, "My grace is sufficient for you, for My strength is made perfect in weakness." Therefore most gladly I will rather boast in my infirmities, that the power of Christ may rest upon me." (2 Corinthians 12:8, 9).

Got it? Jesus wanted him to remain a burned brick! Yes, Saul of Tarsus had transformed into the mighty Apostle Paul. But there was no hiding about where he came from. Despite his everlasting impact on humanity, Jesus asked him to identify with the other burned bricks in the Bible whom God used. Despite the anointing, there was no escape from the reminder in his life that God was building with another burned brick.

Chapter Seven

Wounded Healers

Among the thousands of sermons I have preached in last twenty years, one of the most popular is a message based on Isaiah 53, titled 'Wounded Healers."

Since preaching that God given message, I have come to know of a book by the late Catholic theologian Henri Nouwen titled 'The Wounded Healer.' I have yet to read this book. I am making this public acknowledgement to make it clear that what I am conveying in this chapter is strictly Holy Spirit inspired.

This message came as a revelation to me after realizing that I and my colleagues are called to minister to a wounded generation. Just like in David's household, we see problems in well known Christian homes. The divorce rate among church folks is close to that of the outside world. So many Christian families find themselves embroiled in issues affecting the non-Christians.

Famous Christian leaders like Rev. Jim Cymbala, pastor of Brooklyn Tabernacle and Rev. David Jeremiah, pastor of Shadowbrook Community Church in California has publicly acknowledged struggles in the lives of their children. The struggles in the early life of Franklin Graham are well known.

What surprised me is that God has eventually molded these strugglers into healers! The daughter of Rev. Jim Cymbala is the wife of a pastor now. She and her husband lead a thriving church in New Hampshire, the last I heard. Franklin Graham has become a well known speaker globally, taking the place of his ailing father.

Over the years, as I attend many conferences and listen to the life stories of the speakers, I am astounded at how many of them struggled in their lives before God made them wounded healers. It is this woundedness in their lives that make them approachable, understanding, compassionate and useful.

So we do not need to be ashamed of the wounds in our lives. We are not called to pamper the wounds and sulk about them all our lives. God expect us to take it in boldly, confront it courageously and make them the source of our strength. The life of a wounded healer becomes as exchange point- receiving blows and dispensing healing.

Paul has expressed it the best in 2 Corinthians, chapter 4, and verse 10:

"Always carrying about in the body the dying of the Lord Jesus, that the life of Jesus also may be manifested in our body."

In the pages of the Bible we can see many people who were wounded healers. Jeremiah was a person who was literally wounded many times. He was called as a prophet to his generation as a young lad. God told him, he was separated and consecrated for that office while he was in his mother's womb. We would expect such a person would be greatly appreciated and received with honors.

But that is not what happened to Jeremiah. He was ministering to a generation that did not want to hear words of correction from God. It was also a generation that was filled with corrupted leaders who would prophecy to keep their offices and be on the good side of the king. So they ganged up together against Jeremiah. He had to undergo abuse so many times.

Finally Jeremiah decided that he would not speak in the name of the Lord again. Why should he make enemies? But he could not. The messages that kept coming from the Lord were like 'a fire shut up in his bones.' So he began to speak again and the abuses continued.

When the day Jeremiah forewarned of came to pass, the troops of Babylon came in defeated the Israelites and took their children as captives. How many times god had warned them through Jeremiah;"Why do you want to die in your sins? Turn to me and live." But no one paid any attention.

When this happened Jeremiah was in arrest, his legs locked into a hole bored in a wooden plank. (This was a common practice to control maniacs in the East). Jeremiah was a madman to that generation. So Jeremiah had every reason to sneer at his persecutors and mutter, "You deserve it." But he did not! Eyeing the passing human chain of his fellow countrymen he yelled out, "Don't worry. Your children will come back to their borders."

Why? Jeremiah was a wounded healer!

Another example we can focus on is Apostle Paul. Paul was reluctant to minister in Corinth. God had to strengthen him through a vision to continue to minister there. The ministry was very successful. God did unusual miracles through Paul there. A powerful church was established in Corinth. Yet this is where Paul was questioned the most.

Paul opens up to us in 2 Corinthians more than in any other books he wrote and many intimate things are shared with us. The dichotomy of a wounded healer is given to us in chapters 11 and 12. In chapter 12 Paul tells us the 'more' experiences of his life-"in labors more abundant, in stripes above measure, in prisons more frequently, in deaths often." In chapter 12, Paul introduces himself as 'a man in Christ who fourteen years ago was caught up to the third heaven.' A man who went to the

Paradise and heard inexpressible words, which is not lawful for a man to utter. In Corinth, all the signs of his Apostleship visibly manifested through signs and wonders. Yet, he was rejected by majority in that same church!

That feeling of rejection led him to open up to us and share his deep thoughts. The dichotomy of his wounded healer experience is explained to us in 2 Corinthians, chapter 4, verse 8 onwards.

"We are hard pressed on every side, yet not crushed; we are perplexed, but not in despair; persecuted, but not forsaken; struck down, but not destroyed- always carrying about in the body the dying of the Lord Jesus, that the life of Jesus also may be manifested in our body."

Paul's life became an exchange point- receiving curses and dispensing blessings, receiving blows and dispensing healings, receiving shame and dispensing honor, receiving poverty and dispensing abundance, receiving death and dispensing life.

Even more astounding is what is given to us in chapter 12, verses 7 to 10.

"7 And lest I should be exalted above measure buy the abundance of the revelations, a thorn in the flesh was given to me, a messenger of Satan to buffet me, lest I be exalted above measure.
8 Concerning this thing I pleaded with the Lord three times that it might depart from me.

9 And he said to me, "my grace is sufficient for you, for My strength is made perfect in your weakness." Therefore most gladly I will rather boast in my infirmities, that the power of Christ may rest upon me.
10 Therefore I take pleasure in infirmities, in reproaches, in needs, in persecutions, in distresses, for Christ's sake. For when I am weak, then I am strong."

Look at this again. This is the same Paul by whom God did unusual miracles. Yet when he needed healing, he did not receive it! God promised only grace to continue in the midst of his 'thorn in the flesh.' God asked him to continue to minister as a wounded healer.

Do you know that Jesus Christ himself also is a wounded healer? In John chapter 17, in the midst of his high priestly prayer, twice Jesus asked His father for the glory that He had given to Jesus. But what was given to Him was a cup. Imagine, asking for glory and receiving a cup of wrath.

Why? Not because he did not have glory. His pre-incarnation glory is given to us in Daniel chapter 7. His post resurrection glory is given to us in Revelation chapter 5. No, it was not a question of whether Jesus would re-inherit the glory. The Father was making it clear that the Son will be a wounded healer from that point on.

The second thing that has caught my attention is the amazing prophecy in Zechariah, chapter 12, verse 10.

"And I will pour on the house of David and on the inhabitants of Jerusalem the Spirit of grace and supplication: then they will look on Me whom they pierced."

We understand this prophecy to mean that when Jesus returns to Mount Olive as promised and He raises his hands to bless His people, the Israelites will see the wound marks in his hands and it will help them to realize that this 'pierced one' was always their Messiah.

My problem with this picture is this. I always run to Jesus for my healing. He always heals my inner wounds and exterior wounds. He is still in the healing business. While He was on earth, more than anything else, His ministry was marked by the amazing healing accounts. So how come His wounds are never healed? How come after thousands of years, people will be able to see the wound marks in His hands? Simply because forever He is set apart as a wounded healer!

Even more astounding to me is the passage in Revelation, chapter 19, verses 11 to 14.

11 Now I saw heaven opened, and behold a white horse. And he who sat on him was called Faithful and true, and in righteousness he judges and makes war.
12 His eyes were like a flame of fire, and on his head were many crowns. He had a name written that no one knew except himself.
13 He was clothed with a robe dipped in blood, and his name is called The Word of God.

This is another picture of the return of Jesus Christ. Here he is riding on a white horse wearing many crowns. It is a picture of his kingship. It was common for kings to wear purple. But read the above passage carefully once again. Jesus is not wearing purple in this picture. He is wearing a 'robe dipped in blood.' The book of Revelation repeatedly tells us that all of his followers will be wearing white in heaven. White is a symbol of holiness and it is picture that our holiness will be perfected in heaven. When Jesus returns to earth, the saints will follow Him wearing their white robes. But the one who is riding in the front, 'the captain of our salvation,' alone is not wearing a white robe. We all know that if anyone has a right to wear a white robe, it is Him! Then what happened? Forever he is a wounded healer! Forever He is marked by the blood He shed on the cross!

If our Savior is not ashamed of being a wounded healer and proudly displays it through eternity, why should we be ashamed of our wounds in the past and present? Do not deny the privilege to bring healing to many, because of your own wounds. Let something good come out of it.

Chapter Eight

Less Than Perfect Heroes

When you go down a road that I have taken in this book, there is always a concern that what I am trying to convey through this book may be misunderstood. It is my hope that people will see the truths in these pages that can set them free. My express desire in writing this book is to share the truths I have learned from life experiences and over twenty years of regular Bible studies, to help struggling Christians become overcomers.

One of the central themes in the Bible that has caught our attention again in our day is the concept of 'grace.' Look at the wonderful titles based on grace available in Christian bookstores. Yet, even Paul, the Apostle of Grace, was afraid that some may use it as an excuse to do wicked things. But he could not hold back the truth and has taught us so much on the subject in his epistles.

The Bible is a religious book that portrays its heroes as regular people who struggled like everyone else. But they eventually became great in the sight of men and God, because they refused to give up and stuck it out with God.

Throughout the pages of the Bible, we see this pattern repeated. Both Old Testament heroes and New Testament heroes were the same.

Recently, in a couples Bible study, my wife brought out a point from the life of Abraham. We know Abraham as the father of faith. But he certainly did not start out that way! Yes, he had taken steps of obedience, when he left 'his country, his family and his father's house' to follow the true living God. But by the end of that same chapter (Genesis 12), we see him asking his wife to lie about their relationship to save his neck! He was willing to allow his wife to be a concubine of someone else, after hearing the promise about his progeny at the beginning of the chapter!

Even more astounding is the fact that he repeated the same mistake in Genesis 20, after he heard the specific promise in chapter 18:10, where God told him, "Sarah, your wife shall have a son," despite her old age. We see her ending up in Abimelech's palace.

On both occasions, God had to intervene to keep the sanctity of Sarah's womb. Yet, Sarah turned around and asked Abraham to go and sleep with her maid, so that they can have a child. Abraham obliged and Ismail was the product of that relationship.

Why did they do it?

The only answer we can come up with is the culture from which they came from. Probably it was not a big deal in that culture. Plus it had not still dawned on Abraham and Sarah that they were not product of that previous culture anymore. God had called them out to be the progenitors of a new godly culture, which will bring back God's original rules for mankind (Matthew 19:4).

It took time for them to grow into what God had called them to be. They continuously grew in the grace and knowledge of God and came to a point where Abraham could think of offering his son of promise as a sacrifice, in an act of total obedience.

I have used a whole chapter to discuss the 'growing up struggles' of Jacob. We also know that the names bearers of the twelve tribes of Israel, the twelve sons of Jacob were a messed up bunch. That story of struggle did continue in their history. Very few people were anywhere near perfect. The only exception may be Joseph. Yet, the tribe bearing his son's name, Ephraim, became central in plunging Israel into spiritual darkness.

Look at Solomon, the wisest man on earth! Consider the mistakes in his life!

When we study the leadership of Old Testament Israel, we see very few that single-mindedly served God. Despite his personal failures, that was the bright side of David. He was totally dependent on God all the time.

When we consider the New Testament, we can see again that the leaders were not perfect. Consider the twelve disciples of Jesus. Despite walking with Jesus, they were always squabbling. They were very prejudiced and judgmental. Some of them were very selfish. Two of them openly asked for special privileges in the kingdom. One time they asked Jesus, "What shall we get for leaving everything and following you?" (paraphrased). They all ran away at the trial of Jesus. In the garden of Gethsemane, Jesus asked Peter,"Could you not watch one hour?" (Mark 14:37). The truth is he did not. Even John, who boasted to be the most beloved among the disciples, fell asleep during the most crucial hour in the life of Jesus.

But they all eventually grew in their understanding about Jesus and their place in God's scheme of things. The story of Peter is described elsewhere in this book. In fact, all of the disciples became missionaries who spread the gospel to far away lands and all of them except John died as martyrs for their master. Andrew was crucified at Patras in Achaia (southern Greece). During the persecutions of Herod Agrippa I, King of the Jews, in c AD44, the apostle James was beheaded - 'put to the sword'

(Acts 12:1-2). Philip preached the Gospel in Phrygia (west central Turkey) before dying or being martyred there at Hieropolis. The missionary work of Bartholomew is linked with Armenia (present day Armenia, eastern Turkey, northern Iraq, north western Iran) and India. Other locations include Egypt, Arabia, Ethiopia and Persia (Iran). Traditionally he met his death by being flayed or skinned alive, and then beheaded. Derbent, north of present day Baku on the Caspian Sea may have been his place of martyrdom. Indian Christians from the west coast Kerala area claim they were evangelized by Thomas, who was later speared to death near Madras on the east coast. Mount St. Thomas, close to Madras is associated with his name. Nothing definite is known of Matthew's career. After preaching in Judea, different traditions place his missionary work and possible martyrdom in Ethiopia or Persia. Tradition claims James the Less first worked in Palestine (Israel) before preaching and martyrdom in Egypt. Thaddaeus may have preached in Assyria (eastern Iraq) and Persia (Iran), before joining with Simon the Zealot and being killed with him in Persia.

Even apostle Paul went through a growing process before he became the great apostle.

Read the Bible and see for yourself. God always called less than perfect people and made them great. It was always a process. In between there were periods of struggle and failure in most of their lives. But neither they nor God gave up on them. They overcame whatever was holding them back and became role models for us. So why can't we follow their example?

Remember this always: *Life is not an incident, it is a process.*

Chapter Nine

Crucify Me Upside Down

Nothing encourages a burned brick like a study about the life of the Big Fisherman- Apostle Peter. The man, who was given the keys to the kingdom, was the epitome of human struggles.

We are introduced to Peter rather abruptly in chapter five of the Gospel of Luke. One day Jesus was giving a public discourse on the shores of the sea of Galilee and when the multitude started pressing Him, Jesus just stepped into the boat of Peter and asked him to move the boat a little into the water. Probably Jesus wanted to use the water as a natural amplifier of his voice so that the huge crowd can hear Him better. But it also was an opportunity for Peter to listen to Jesus while he was busy fixing his fishing net.

When the discourse was over, the events took a different turn than Peter ever expected. Jesus started giving him advice about fishing! Peter was astounded. But something had happened to Peter already. Listening to Jesus that day, Peter realized that this was no ordinary Rabbi. So he responded in obedience testifying to His emerging faith in Jesus. The ensuing catch multiplied his faith many times over and he had no trouble to believe that his destiny was to become a 'catcher of men'. So he and his partners, the sons of Zebedee, left their boats and nets and even the huge catch of the day and followed Jesus.

The three and half years of following Jesus were eventful in the life of Peter. There were many ups and downs. The most poignant moment was when he received the revelation about Jesus as recorded in the Gospel of Matthew, chapter 16. It brought a tremendous promise from Jesus into his life.

> "And I also say to you that you are Peter, and on this rock I will build My church, and the gates of Hades shall not prevail against it.
> "I will give you the keys of the kingdom of heaven and whatever you bind on earth will be bound in heaven, and whatever you loose on earth will be loosed in heaven." (Matthew 16:18, 19)

Yet, a few minutes later Peter's humanity was in full view. Despite the revelation, he was used by Satan to question the plans of God. The same Jesus, who pronounced tremendous blessings over Peter, ended up rebuking him.

Peter became the leader among the disciples. Yet, he had his down times. One time Peter boasted that he was willing to die with Jesus. Hearing it, Jesus told Peter about how Satan had asked for him, to sift him like wheat. (Luke 22:31). Peter did not even know about it! Many times we are like Peter. When we boast about many things, we do not know half the things that are going on-in the natural or in the supernatural. Jesus did not allow Satan to sift Peter 'that his faith should not fail.'

Then Jesus told him about the coming temptation. He predicted that this same Peter, who loved Jesus enough to die with Him, will deny Jesus three times before the cock crow twice during the night of crucifixion. Peter probably laughed in denial. No way!

His bravado in the garden of Gethsemane was impressive. It looked for a moment that he meant what he said earlier: that he would die with Jesus. But then he ran away like all the other disciples. Later that night as he hung around to know what would happen to Jesus, the prediction of Jesus was sadly fulfilled. He did deny Jesus three times that night.

What happened in between must be noted here. When Jesus took James, John and Peter to the garden of Gethsemane, it was as prayer partners. It was also an occasion for Peter to take victory through prayer. Jesus told them, "Pray that you may not enter into temptation." (Luke 22:39). But they slept anyway.

After the first round of prayer, Jesus came back to them and found them sleeping. Jesus specifically addressed Peter and asked him, "Simon, are you sleeping? Could you not watch one hour?" (Mark 14:37). Jesus warned him again, "Watch and pray, lest you enter into temptation." (Mark 14:38). It did not strike Peter that Jesus was giving him a way of victory. So he continued to sleep until it was too late. Thus it is no wonder that he was powerless to stand before a servant girl.

When Jesus looked at him after the cock crew the third time, it spoke volumes to Peter. It was a moment of truth for Peter. He finally could see through himself. Despite the bravado, despite the zealous attitude, he realized he was powerless. He did not think Jesus could use him again.

So despite meeting the resurrected Jesus many times, he left the 'ministry.' One day he told his friends that he was going back to fishing. Because he was their leader, they decided to go with him (John 21:3). He was backsliding out of frustration.

Jesus had to come back to the sea of Tiberius (which is same as the Sea of Galilee), where he had originally climbed into the boat of Peter, to fetch him and restore him in faith. Talk about grace!

When Jesus started talking to him, Peter was brushing things off. We know this from the words being used. When Jesus asked Peter, "Simon, son of Jonah, do you love (*agapao*) Me more than these?" he was trying to find out where was Peter's heart. Peter used the word '*phileo*' when he replied to Jesus. The modern rendition may be, "Yeah, I still like you." The warmth of the love of God was not there. The third time when

Jesus asked him the same question, Jesus changed the word to 'phileo.' That is when Peter broke down. All he could say was, "Lord, You know all things!" That is the answer Jesus wanted to hear. He knew how disappointed Peter was with his conduct, how disappointed he was for letting himself and others down, how disappointed he was for denying Jesus etc. He just wanted Peter to confess it. Jesus spoke into his life again and restored him and commanded him, "Follow Me," which was the original command to Peter.

Once restored in faith, Peter took up his place. He was the leader of the group of disciples on the day of Pentecost. He was the one who addressed the crowd. He saw over three thousand people joining the church after his first message. Miracles began to happen in his ministry. It reached a point where his mere shadow could bring healing to people.

All the promises about his life came to pass. He used the keys to the kingdom given to him by Jesus to open the door for Jewish believers to enter the kingdom on the day of Pentecost. In the same manner, at the house of Cornelius, he opened the kingdom for the gentiles.

Tradition tells us that he visited many churches and ministered in many cities as the leader of Christianity. At the end of his life, he was crucified. His only request was to be crucified upside down, since he was not worthy to die like his Master after denying Him.

Take courage from Peter's life account. If Jesus would restore a person who denied Him, after walking with Him and talking with Him for three and a half years, after being an eye witness to everything Jesus did (who in fact became the primary source for the synoptic (first three) Gospels we have in the Bible), will He not restore you, if you truly repent of your sins and come to Him for restoration? No sinner is beyond salvation and no backslider is beyond restoration! We can be confident like Apostle Paul that 'He who has begun a good work in you will complete it until the day of Jesus Christ.' (Philippians 1:6)

Chapter Ten

Let The Stump Remain

One of the beautiful pictures of God's faithfulness is found in the book of Daniel. I am not referring to the blessings that Daniel or his friends received from the Lord. It is the life of Nebuchadnezzar, a gentile king.

I know that the presentation in the Bible is different from that of secular history. Secular historians look at Nebuchadnezzar as the most prominent emperor of Neo- Babylon empire, who rose to power in the natural course of history. Many do not even acknowledge that a Jew named Daniel had significant influence in the empire or played a key role there during the reign of Nebuchadnezzar. A lot of people have difficulty accepting the book of Daniel as it is (because the prophecies were fulfilled accurately).

However, as a Christian author, I am very interested in what the Bible has to say about things. And what the Bible presents in reference to Nebuchadnezzar is nothing short of amazing.

In Jeremiah, chapter 25, verse 9 and chapter 27, verse 6, God calls Nebuchadnezzar, 'His servant'. It was part of God's plan to raise up Nebuchadnezzar into a powerful position and use him to teach a lesson to God's people, the Israel, who had gone away from the Lord. Just as God had a plan to eradicate the addiction to idol worship from the Israelites through the Babylonian captivity, God had also worked out how they will be preserved during that time period, who will lead them into captivity and who will lead them out of captivity. The entire episode is a classical study in God's faithfulness and God's omnipotence.

Thus, according to Bible, despite being a gentile king, Nebuchadnezzar was an instrument in God's hand. What blew me away is realizing that God showed the same longsuffering with him as with His chosen people.

The first encounter Nebuchadnezzar had with God was when he saw the dream about a huge statue made with different metals. Later we read in the book of Daniel that he saw that dream, while he was worried about the future of his kingdom. One reason for the worry was that his follower on his throne was his son in law, not his son. As the person responsible for expanding the tiny kingdom into a vast empire, he was naturally worried about the future of it and his place in history.

In order to assure him, God showed him a dream, through the interpretation of which, god made it clear to him that his place in history is secure as 'the head of the statue.' In other words, God told him that a new era in human history was beginning with him and that the chain of events will not interrupt until Christ come and establish His kingdom on earth. So, hundreds of thousands of students of the prophecy in history, in their analysis to understand how things played out the way it did, will trace back the history to him, The Babylonian captivity of Israel is a topic of study until today. How amazing was the rest of the interpretation by Daniel that accurately foretold the arrival of Medo-Persian, Greek and Roman empires on the scene. Then it also foretold how the last chapter of human history will play out.

In other words, when Nebuchadnezzar was just worried about the immediate future, an all knowing God, told him much more using a dream, and assured him that his place in history was safe. Like most of the people who unexpected receive a blessing from God, he was grateful and acknowledged that "truly your God [is] the God of gods, the Lord of kings, and a revealer of secrets, since you could reveal this secret." (Daniel 2:47)

But he did not want anything to do with this God! He continued serving his own plethora of gods. In this Nebuchadnezzar is just like millions in the world today. They will call upon the true living God in times of need and will be even grateful for His blessings. But they refuse to serve Him!

We are shocked initially to see in the next chapter of Daniel, Nebuchadnezzar erecting a huge statue of his own and asking people to worship him as god. Two things are clear here. One, Nebuchadnezzar did not accept the assurance from God that his place in history is safe. He still felt that he needed to make sure of it. So, he in his vanity, thought if he erected a statue that is 90 feet high, covered with gold, that will be his eternal memorial. Isn't it funny that the whole world talk about the hanging gardens of Babylon but nobody, except the students of Bible, talks about the statue! (It is a lesson in itself for all of us. The hanging gardens of Babylon were planted for Nebuchadnezzar's wife Amytis, whereas the statue was a shameless display of his vanity. So our real memorial is what we do for others, not what we do to display ourselves).

This display of vanity led to the second encounter with God. Nebuchadnezzar threatened to throw into fire anyone who will refuse to worship him. Three Jewish boys named Shadrach, Meshach, and Abed-Nego refused to oblige, because worshipping an idol was against the second commandment. The king became very angry and threw them into the fire as he had threatened. Then he, not others, saw the incredible sight of the same boys walking in the fire unharmed along with a fourth person, whom Nebuchadnezzar called 'the Son of God.' What a revelation for a gentile king!

It shows clearly that King Nebuchadnezzar knew God in his heart, even though he was walking in disobedience and rebellion, just like so many people we know.

Again he had a temporary repentance and declared
"Blessed be the God of Shadrach, Meshach, and Abed-Nego, who sent His Angel and delivered His servants who trusted in Him, and they have frustrated the king's word, and yielded their bodies, that they should not serve nor worship any god except their own God!

Therefore I make a decree that any people, nation, or language which speaks anything amiss against the God of Shadrach, Meshach, and Abed-Nego shall be cut in pieces, and their houses shall be made an ash heap; because there is no other God who can deliver like this." (Daniel 3:28,29)

Look at his word carefully. Even after this second encounter with the living God, though he acknowledges Him and accepts that there is no other God like this, there is no personal commitment to serve Him! He gives more religious freedom to the Jews and that is it. But God's purpose was to bring Nebuchadnezzar to a point of surrender to His plans for him. Like, so many thousands of proud men and women, he refused and tried to escape by playing the 'religious card.'

God who do not repent of His calling was not through with him. Just as myself and many other s have learned in life, there is only o far you can run from God. Many times God is like a fisherman who has the fish hooked up on his line, yet let the line run for a while. The fish may think that it is escaping by all the wiggling, but eventually the fish will be reeled in!

Oh how many troubles we could have avoided if we are ready t listen to God, when He speaks to us in various ways! It is unimaginable that a gentile person who had two crystal clear encounters with God would not turn to Him! Or, is it?

We force the hand of God to deal with us more forcefully when we refused to listen to His gentle dealings.
Paul talked about it as 'despising the riches of His goodness, forbearance, and longsuffering, not knowing that the goodness of God leads one to repentance'. (Romans 2:4)

Psalm 107 has a portion that talks directly about such people.
Those who sat in darkness and in the shadow of death, Bound in affliction and irons--
Because they rebelled against the words of God, And despised the counsel of the Most High,
Therefore He brought down their heart with labor; They fell down, and [there was] none to help.
Then they cried out to the LORD in their trouble, [And] He saved them out of their distresses.
He brought them out of darkness and the shadow of death, And broke their chains in pieces.
Oh, that [men] would give thanks to the LORD [for] His goodness, And [for] His wonderful works to the children of men!
For He has broken the gates of bronze, And cut the bars of iron in two. (Psalms 107:10-16)

Nebuchadnezzar's refusal to yield to God's revealed plan for his life led to a third encounter with God. This time it was so bad that you would not wish it upon your enemies even! The account Is given to us in Daniel, chapter four. It was included in the original copy of Daniel in Aramaic to show the authenticity of this incredible account.

The summary of the account is this. Nebuchadnezzar continued to refuse to give glory to God- for his elevation or his place in history. So God showed him another vision. Again, we see him going to the magicians and Chaldeans instead of calling in Daniel, whom he knew had a 'divine spirit' in him, according to the king's own confession. But calling in Daniel will be acknowledging God again. And the king did not want to do that!

Once again Daniel had to enter the scene to receive the divine interpretation. It was so shocking that the king had to cajole Daniel to make him utter it.

The dream was of a mighty tree that had spread branches all around under which many of the beasts and the birds were seeking refuge. It was a clear picture of Nebuchadnezzar's empire. But then came the decree to cut the tree down for a period of seven 'times.' At the same time God promised to *leave the stump and roots in the earth, bound with a band of iron and bronze.* (Daniel 4:15).

Daniel told the king that the dream was a forewarning from God about the impending humiliation from God. The decree was this:

Let him be drenched with the dew of heaven, and let him live with the animals among the plants of the earth. Let his mind be changed from that of a man and let him be given the mind of an animal, till seven times pass by for him (Daniel 4: 15, 16).

It was to teach the king forcefully that
"the Most High rules in the kingdom of men,
Gives it to whomever He will,
And sets over it the lowest of men."(Daniel 4:17)

This lesson was not new. God told him the same thing in Daniel chapter 2, in the interpretation of the dream about the statue. But he continued to refuse it. So God decided to remove King Nebuchadnezzar from the throne in a most humiliating way for a period of 'seven times.' Seven times in Bible is usually seven years. The king would have a mental breakdown and would be acting as a beast and even grass from the field. Daniel concluded by advising the king to turn from wickedness (of unbelief) and to show kindness to the poor so that the 'tranquility may remain.'

God, despite pronouncing the judgment, gave the king twelve months to turn his life around. He did not and all the peace and tranquility was gone from Babylon.

When the image fiasco did not work, he went on a building binge and turned the city of Babylon into an architectural marvel. Then when it was done, one day he proclaimed to himself,

"Is not this great Babylon, that I have built for a royal dwelling by my mighty power and for the honor of my majesty?" (Daniel 4:30)

Archaeologists have discovered an inscription with interesting parallels to what Daniel reports Nebuchadnezzar to have said about himself in Daniel 4:30. This inscription has been found in Babylon what is known as the East India House Inscription. On this inscription is included a statement credited to Nebuchadnezzar, In Babylon, my dear city, which I love, was the palace, the house of wonder of the people, the bond of the land, the brilliant place, the abode of the majesty in Babylon. Another Babylonian inscription with parallels to Daniel 4:30 is known as the Grotefend Cylinder. On this cylinder is found the statement in Nebuchadnezzar's name, "Then I built the palace, the seat of my royalty, the bond of the race of men, the dwelling of joy and rejoicing. These are two more bricks in the wall which prove the historical reliability of Daniel. (Source: evidenceforchritianity.org)

The judgment was swift. The same night of this proud proclamation, King Nebuchadnezzar's mind flipped and he started acting the way God said he would. It continued for seven years. Then just as amazingly God restored his mind and his kingdom and majesty returned to him.

A number of aspects amaze us as we ponder this incident. First of all, the most insecure thing in the world was a king's throne, sine so many others wanted it. Thus, it is amazing to read that despite the king acting as a lunatic and living on the place lawn, instead of inside the palace, his throne was there when his mind was restored! It does not happen in history! What happened here?

God promised to 'let the stump remain, bound with bronze and iron.' In effect God said this:"I am going to cur this proud tree down because he does not learn his lessons or yield to My will for his life. My intention is not to destroy him, but to turn him around. It will take seven years of humiliation and suffering for his pride to break down and for him to turn around. But, nonetheless, I will protect him during that time period. I know that many will come to finish him off, seeing that the tree is cut down by Me. Many will try to take the stump out of the ground to finalize the chapter of destruction in his life and usher themselves in his place. But I will not let it happen. I will protect the stump, though it looks dry and withered, exposed to elements and destined for rotting. I will protect the stump since I have plans to let it flourish again, after this time of correction is over in his life. I will protect the stump since I have plans to restore his glory. I will protect the stump since I have plans to restore him to respectability."

Oh, how many of us can shout amen to that! Isn't that the life story of thousands among us? We are here, restored and doing well, only because God allowed the stump to remain, while we were going through the time of correction in our lives. How much we should praise the faithfulness of God, for guarding the stumps of our lives with bronze and iron, while so many others thought it was over and they wanted to dig up the stump and get it over with?

Secondly, it is unimaginable that a king would write down this kind of shameful incidents in his life and will send it to all the provinces and 'unto all peoples.' Especially when you remember that this was a king obsessed with his legacy. It is the beauty of the liberty in Christ. One Jesus sets us free from our obsessions, addictions and other destructive behaviors, we are free indeed. There comes a new found courage to talk about the worst times in your life- not to glory in the gory, but to use it as an example for many to learn lessons from. Some of you may be in the season of correction in your life. You may be reading this book in the confines of a jail cell. But do not worry. If God has plan for your life, which He has, He will allow the stump to remain so that you can have a fruitful send part to your life where you can testify of the faithfulness of God just like King Nebuchadnezzar. Do not be ashamed of your correction period(s). If a kin can write it down and send it all the provinces in his empires that others may learn from his life experiences, your testimony also can be a powerful tool to turn many to the righteousness of God.

Thirdly, God accomplished what he wanted to do. It was a very costly lesson for King Nebuchadnezzar, which he could have avoided if he had listened to the advice of Daniel. Yet, the result was forever a glorious testimony of God's faithfulness.

Finally Nebuchadnezzar was ready for a personal relationship with a living God. He concludes his testimony with these words:

"Now I, Nebuchadnezzar, praise and extol and honor the King of heaven, all of whose works [are] truth, and His ways justice. And those who walk in pride He is able to put down." (Daniel 4:37).

Are you ready to surrender your life like this mighty king and start a personal relationship with the true living God? The door is open to you through the death of His only begotten Son, Jesus Christ. He is ready to receive you. He promises, 'the one who comes to Me I will by no means cast out.' (John 6:37) Do it today.

Chapter Eleven

Overcoming Childhood Traumas

Only after I got into my forties did I realize that the most important period in a person's life is childhood. The childhood experiences determines who we are, how we will react to situations, what kind of personality we have as adults, how we will succeed in our careers, marriage and life in general. I believe that is why there is so much attack on childhood and things that are important to children. Even if you are not a believer in God, you have to wonder why so many children have to go through what they endure.

Oftentimes, it is also easy for children to conclude in their little minds that what they went through in life is natural. Moreover, they are busy growing up and enchanted by the endless things opening up before them that they do not have time like the adults to sulk and complain.

So, our childhood experiences actually become more important to us in our adulthood. Even if you did not complain or even admitted the bad things that happened to you in your childhood; it shapes your thinking, your attitudes, your relationships and in many cases your success in life.

I know this because I have been there. I had very loving parents. Yet, my father's work forced us to live in different places during my childhood. I had to attend five different schools to graduate from high school. That regular uprooting forced us to find new friends. Some of them were good and some were bad. It put me in many unexpected situations at a young age, to which I never paid any attention until I was forced to reflect on my childhood later.

I had the stability provided by a loving church since a young age. I was good in studies and enjoyed the love and respect of teachers. So I never paid any attention to the occasional abuse and damage done to my psyche. I was an extremely curios student, always interested in reading whatever book I could find in the village library or in someone's home and learning about 'everything under the sun.'

However, in my late thirties, I began to notice that I had some issues. All of a sudden there was a cloud hanging over my life. The solid single-mindedness started missing in me and I always wondered why. It is something I admired much and always tried to develop. I always noticed that quality in my hero, Jesus Christ- always knowing what He wanted to do in a given situation and sticking to His plan in the midst of overwhelming odds. It is the trait I admired most in a leader. In short, I realized that I was not the person I thought I was- always sure, always confident.

That was a horrible day! I felt like the tin lion in the Wizard of Oz- projecting an aura of greatness while being shallow inside.

As always, I began to spend time in the presence of God to find answers. One of the things the spirit of God did was to lead me to a study in the life of David. Talk about contradictions! Despite his greatness, there was always what I call an 'easy-to-fall-in-the-pit'ness to his life. He was a tremendous worshipper, a person who truly loved God and eventually became 'a man after God's own heart.' But in his personal life, he struggled mightily. His struggles as a father are all over the story. As a warrior he was mighty. As a worshipper, he was glorious. He was the sweet poet of Israel. He was a king whose reputation spread to all the neighboring countries. So much to be proud of in his life! Yet, his personal life was full of struggles. By the end of my study, I had no doubt left in me that those struggles were the product of his childhood.

Usually the youngest in the house is the baby of the house, showered with special love and care to the extent of spoiling them. But David was shoved out of the home to take care of the household sheep. My interpretation is that David's tinkering with musical instruments all day long was too much for his elderly parents and they found a convenient way to get to rid of him! When Samuel showed up at his home with God's commission to anoint one of the children of Jesse as the next king in Israel, his parents did not even consider him! Samuel had to ask them pointedly, "Are here all your children?" Are you sure that you haven't forgotten anyone? Only then did his father remember that he had another son!

David later wrote about his experiences this way: "When my father and mother forsake me, then the LORD will take me up." (Psalms 27:10). This is the Psalm where David declared, "The LORD is my light and my salvation, whom shall I fear? The LORD is the strength of my life, of whom shall I be afraid?"

In a nutshell, David is a man of God who struggled for many years before truly becoming a man after God's own heart. David's life was a classic case where life pushed him into the lime light without being nurtured for it.

As I conclude this small book, I believe it is the same situation with many of my readers. Many of my early years in ministry were with the young people. During that time, I came across so many talented and gifted kids who simply could not put the pieces together and excel consistently. I always used to wonder why. I wished I had figured out *then* the things I am sharing with you in this book *now*.

Today I have no doubt that a rotten childhood is at the center of many of the problems that adults face. Many young people rot in jail not knowing how they ended up there. Statistics show that many of them come from broken or single parent homes. How can we expect children to have a life long relationship with their partners, if the parents slipped out of their marriage vows for the simplest of reasons and did not care for children properly? Many of their children have ruined their marriages without any willful malice towards their partners. They simply do not know why they mess up. If they allow God to open their eyes and are willing to confront the hard facts of life, they can be healed and live fruitful and productive lives.

There is a three step process that will help you to accomplish this: *acknowledge, forgive and move forward.* (Once again, I am not a psychologist and do not take this advice to replace professional advice, if you need it. What I suggest is a process that the Holy Spirit illuminated in my mind while I was trying to help myself and others. I know it works for a child of God.)

It takes courage to acknowledge things. Your childhood experiences are settled somewhere in the bottom of your mind and has become part of the sediments there. It is not easy to stir them up again. You may become hundreds of times more emotional now than in your childhood, if those memories are stirred up. Now that you are an adult, you can analyze it more and the pain can be greater. But you have to do it to receive inner healing. After receiving the healing, you can leave it covered by the blood of the Lamb forever. It will be truly behind you.

As a Christian, you have to forgive the person(s) responsible for your traumas. Many of them may be dead already. If they are alive, deal with it biblically. The Bible teaches us to forgive our enemies. Forgiveness is a very powerful tool. Once you forgive a person, you are no longer held captive by that person. You are liberated to move on with your life. That is why Jesus emphasized and practiced forgiveness so much.

However it is good to confront the person(s) who inflicted you the pain and let them know that you are *choosing* to forgive them because you are a Christian. This way you will not feel later that it was an act of weakness on your part.

We must move forward. We should not waste our lives pampering old wounds forever. To use your childhood as an excuse for continuous failure in life will be a mistake. It does no one any good. Once you realize that there were issues and incidents in your childhood that has affected your personality and has caused issues later in adult life, muster the courage to deal with it. Refuse to be a victim forever. By acknowledging, confronting and forgiving, one gets a second chance in life. One should move forward with a vengeance, redeeming the time he or she has left on earth, serving both man and God.

Yes, the burned marks may be there on your life- both visible and invisible. But it does not have to stop you from reaching your destiny!

When we read through the seven letters given to seven churches in the book of Revelation, we see that the rewards are given to the 'overcomers.' The Bible does not use the word 'victorious.' The word used is 'overcomers.' What is the difference? Overcomers are people who became victorious in the end! They are people who 'made it' despite everything life, the world and Satan stacked up against them. They had struggles, but they overcame. They had failures, but they overcame. They had issues, but they overcame. People were betting against them, but they overcame. They have wound marks to show for the struggles in life, but they are victorious in the end!

Like Apostle Paul, forget the things behind and aim for the goal ahead of you. God who created you for His purposes will fulfill them and you will be victorious in the end.

Rise up and march forward into your destiny!

Chapter Twelve

No More Defeat

Now that you have hopefully got a grip on your situation and your life and have addressed them in the light of the word of God, you must accept your place in God's scheme of things and take steps to redeem the rest of the time you have on this earth. You should not waste another moment walloping in self pity. God has forgiven your mistakes and you have asked forgiveness from the people you have offended. Or in some cases, you have confronted the people who have wounded you and told them that you are forgiving them as a child of God. After these steps you are ready to move on in life. One thought you should have at this point must be how to make sure that cycle of failures will not repeat in your life. The following thoughts can help you in this area.

In James chapter 1, we read two references to tests. KJV uses the word 'temptation' for both. But they are a world apart. Simpler translations like NLT make it very clear. In v.2 and 3, he refers to the trials of faith they were going through. It was definitely a reference to the persecution against the early church. He tells the believers that those trials are precious and that they can have victory through patience. Though the church lost thousands because of the persecution that lasted through the fourth century, she did maintain her patience and came out victorious.

But what is referred to in v. 13 to 15 is entirely different. I like the candid rendition in NLT: "And remember, no one who wants to do wrong should ever say, 'God is tempting me.'"

Remember that this was written to Jewish Christians scattered among the nations. Why we as Christians have to worry about temptations? Do any of us really want to do wrong? Or are we destined to lose some battles in life?

Why do we lose the battles is the question. After going through the 'new creation' experience at salvation (2 Cor.5:17), after committing ourselves to 'walk in the newness of life' at baptism (Romans 6:4), after receiving the power to be 'victorious witnesses' by the infilling of the Holy Spirit (Acts 1:8), why we still have to worry about stumbling and defeat?

The simple answer to that is that we are still in our mortal bodies that we inherited at birth. This body came with the Adamic sin nature. As long as we are in this body, therefore, there will be a dichotomy in the life of a Christian. This is why Paul cried out for divine intervention in Romans 7.

A detailed study on this subject would warrant writings by holiness and puritan writers of America. John Wesley has written extensively on the subject of holiness.

One does not have to live a defeated life. He or she can have victory if you do the following:

1. Accept certain realities.

Even a Christian can be lured by evil desires. As long as we are in this body, only our souls are saved. We still live in a body that has carnal desires. I have heard the story of an eighty five old mother in church who was approached by young ladies. They asked her:"Mother, how old was you when you finally got over all the carnal desires in your life?" Her answer was to go and ask someone older than her! We have two laws at work in a Christian as Paul teaches us in Romans 7. One law that is the product of the new creation in Christ that wants to 'conform to the image of the Son.' The other law came to us as an inheritance through the lineage of Adam. It is not fun to be in battle field- whether your battle field is Iraq or it is your mind. Even Apostle Paul cried out," O wretched man that I am! Who will deliver me from this body of death?" What he is saying is that this battle will go on until death. But despite the struggle one can have victory if one does not give in.

2. Treat every temptation as a test of your faith.

Tests can come in different forms. Like Odysseus in Greek mythology, we may think that we are beyond temptation. But no one is! Just as his soldiers had to tie him to the mast to save him, we need intervention in such times to protect our Christian walk. But from whom? Read on.

3. God has made provisions to help you.

In Hebrews chapter 2, v. 18 and chapter 4, v.15, the Bible assures us that our savior Jesus Christ understands perfectly what we go through because he was living among us for 33 plus years. That is why Paul cried out: "Thank God! The answer is in Jesus Christ our Lord." (Rom. 7:25 NLT). He has promised us that he will never leave us or forsake us. That goes for the times when you are severely struggling in your faith also.

4. There is a way of escape.

What I have learned from experience and from the Word of God is that Satan cannot defeat a Christian until he or she gives up. Many times Satan will increase the fire seven times to force you to give up. But if you hold on to your convictions, you will be walking free in that fire a short time later! Learn this secret:

Many times having victory is as simple as buying a little extra time. A simple 'not now' can lead you to victory a million times!

5. Put on the whole armor of God.

Spiritual warfare is a reality! There is only one way to victory in that area. Get ready for the fight! Put on the armor God has provided for you in Ephesians 6:10-16. "Resist the devil and he will flee away."

Make up your mind. Proclaim to yourself: No More Defeat!

I have a maker
He formed my heart,
before even time began
My life was in his hands

He knows my name
He knows my every thought,
He sees each tear that falls
and hears me when I call

I have a father,
he calls me his own
He'll never leave me,
no matter where I go

He knows my name
He knows my every thought
He sees each tear that falls
and hears me when I call

He knows my name
He knows my every thought
He sees each tear that falls
And hears me when I call
He hears me when I call
-Paul Baloche

Forthcoming books by Dr. Sunny Philip

1.   Passion for God.

A book filled with insights that will help you to rekindle your passion and faith as a Christian.

2.   The Search for Meaning of Life.

An in depth study in the book of Ecclesiastes comparing the ancient wisdom with the experiences of the modern man.

3.   Become a Person After God's Own Heart

In depth studies in the life of David that will transform your life and set you on a course to reach the destiny for which you were created.

These books will be available from:

Amazon.com

Sphilip.org

Gatewaynyc.com

Made in the USA
Charleston, SC
25 November 2009